$3.95

D0099472

JohnDenver

text **Charles and Ann Morse**
illustrations **John Keely**
design concept **Mark Landkamer**

published by **Creative Education**
Mankato, Minnesota

Published by Creative Educational Society, Inc.,
123 South Broad Street, Mankato, Minnesota 56001
Copyright © 1975 by Creative Educational Society, Inc. International
copyrights reserved in all countries.
No part of this book may be reproduced in any form without written permission
from the publisher. Printed in the United States.
Distributed by Childrens Press, 1224 West Van Buren Street, Chicago, Illinois 60607
Library of Congress Number: 74-14551   ISBN: 0-87191-392-5

Library of Congress Cataloging in Publication Data
Morse, Charles.   John Denver.
SUMMARY: A brief biography stressing the professional career of
singer and songwriter, John Denver.
1. Denver, John—Juvenile lit. [1. Denver, John. 2. Singers, American]
I. Morse, Ann, joint author. II. Keely, John, illus. III. Title.
ML3930.D42M7   784,4'92'4 [B] [93]   74-14551
ISBN 0-87191-392-5

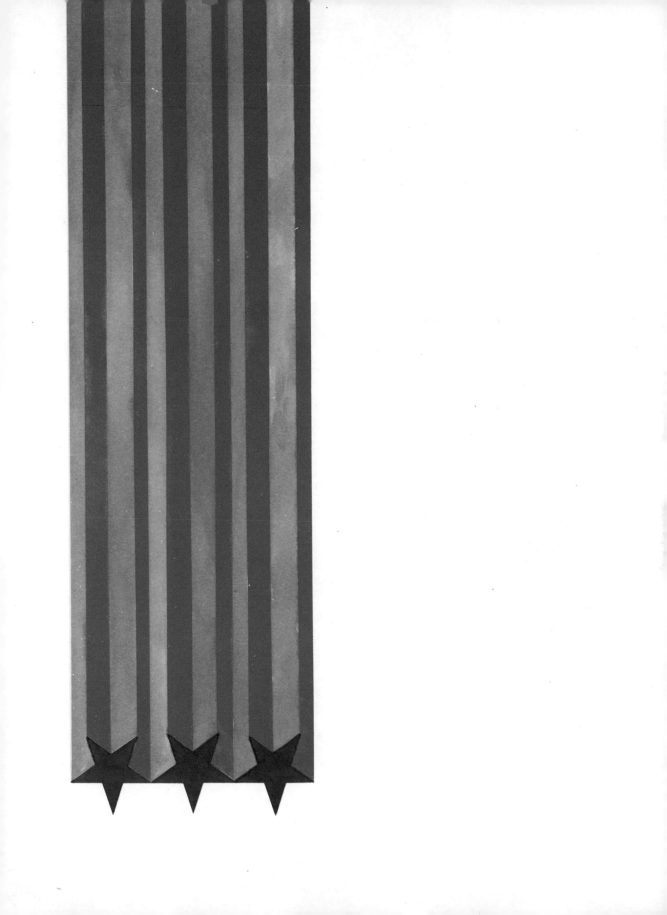

Nearly 20,000 people pushed their way into the concert hall, hurrying to escape the chill of a damp spring night. The crowd was a mixture of young and old, short and long hair, patched jeans and business suits. The push grew stronger. In minutes John Denver would be appearing in a 1974 spring concert in St. Paul, Minnesota.

A Happy Man

People scrambled to find assigned seats in the huge hall. Technicians tested lights and adjusted sound equipment. Musicians tuned their instruments. An air of professionalism filled the concert hall. Giant heaters blew warm breezes over the chilled crowd. Night came as the lights dimmed.

As John Denver began to sing, 20,000 listeners seemed drawn into a small circle of warmth around a magical campfire. Behind Denver were 3 large screens. Suddenly these screens came alive with pictures of blue skies, snow falling down mountain slopes, a campfire in the Rocky Mountain wilderness. Music, lights, slides and films caught hold of John Denver's spirit. In seconds the spirit had spread to the people gathered there.

On that cool evening in St. Paul, the sellout crowd was momentarily transported to the top of a mountain. John Denver was singing "The Eagle and the Hawk." As he sang, the screen showed an eagle and a hawk swirling about and hanging under clouds. For an instant the listeners were caught up in the beauty of the flight. A 24-piece orchestra plus Denver's 5 permanent sidemen, helped to bring the song to a moving, soaring point.

Then on the center screen, in slow motion a flower opened. Water rushed over rocks. And John Denver, holding onto his leather hat, ran down the mountainside. One of the slide screens showed a picture of John's face, wearing a large smile. In front of it all the performer sang,

"Sunshine on my shoulder makes me happy."

Some artists sing of cold things. Other artists sing in the warmth of the sun. John Denver is an artist of the sun.

John Denver has felt the cold of rainy days, the chill of a March wind, the hardness of rocks under bare feet. But John Denver chooses sunshine over rain, warm over cold, soft over hard.

People who know him offstage say he's just John — warm-hearted, grinning, sincere. He's a songwriter and performer who feels the warmth of life. It's a definite part of Denver's campfire-style concerts.

John Denver's songs make people happy. At his concerts Denver wants people to feel good, not about him, but about themselves. "People come to my shows to get turned on about themselves, not me," Denver once said. "Still, I try to be myself on stage," he added. John is just the way he seems to be. John Denver is a joyful musician.

Many rock musicians say it isn't "hip" to be happy today. It's more cool, some say, to show anger or to be irritating in songs. Critics call Denver "Mr. Clean" and the "Mickey Mouse of Rock." But critics can't touch his spirit.

Denver once related an incident which shows his self-confidence in what he is about. In the early 1970s John was performing at a campus show. During the intermission a group came backstage and demanded that Denver sing a song they had written against the war. John asked them how long their protest group had been in existence. When one of them said 4 days, John said, "Look, I've been singing protest songs for 6 years." John excused the incident as a spring-fever thing.

John went on to tell the same interviewer that he feels it is people, not groups, who really make changes. And it is in the little things where change happens. "In traffic, in grocery stores, you let somebody else in front of you. That's peace," John said. "You have to have some consideration for the things around you. Then, there is joy, great joy in life."

"I want to communicate the joy I have in living or in loving someone," Denver responds to his critics. "Life is all we have," he adds. John believes in life. And he believes people can be happy in life. John's beliefs are behind almost every song he sings.

Storyteller

Balladeer, troubadour, druid — John Denver is all of these. John is a druid in the way his songs work magic in making people feel good. He is like the troubadours of long ago, singing his romantic stories as he strolls through life. Like a balladeer, Denver makes up ballads in verse and rhyme. John Denver is all these things because he is a storyteller.

A storyteller draws a circle around people's lives, connecting the past, the present and the future. A storyteller makes it all one.

Many of John's songs reflect one of the biggest things in his own life, saying good-bye. Throughout his life, John has spent so much time on the road that he has become very good at writing songs of farewell. "Leaving, on a Jet Plane" and "Follow Me" were Denver's first hits.

When John was a child, he had to get used to moving often. He can't forget his childhood. As he records and performs on the road now, John carries with him the memories of past journeys.

Henry John Deutschendorf, Jr., which is Denver's real name, was born in Roswell, New Mexico, on December 31, 1943. Since John's father was a jet pilot in the Air Force, his family had to move wherever he was stationed.

John and his younger brother, Ronald, grew up in New Mexico, Oklahoma, Arizona, Alabama, Texas and Florida. They even spent 3 years in Japan.

John has often spoken about those early years of his life. "I had kind of a lonely childhood," he said. "We never stayed any place long enough to make friends."

When John was in the seventh grade, his grandmother gave him a 1910 Gibson guitar. The guitar helped him to make friends. John was too small to be good in competitive sports. Because he was naturally shy, it was difficult for him to make friends. But the guitar gave him something to do with friends.

John took his guitar everywhere. He can still remember how he felt, standing in the lunch line with his guitar. When kids would ask him whether he could play it, John made sure that they were glad they had asked.

Throughout high school, John continued to let his guitar and songs do some of his talking for him. During the summers, John went to his uncle's farm in Oklahoma. He would compose songs as he drove the tractor or rode the combine.

John's parents encouraged his musical interests. Though the family had to move often, John and Ronald felt secure. Erma and Henry Deutschendorf gave their sons much love and taught them to trust and to believe in people.

When John graduated from Arlington Heights High

School in Fort Worth, Texas, his parents gave him an electric guitar. They hoped he would enter the Air Force Academy, but John was rejected for nearsightedness. He then entered Texas Tech University to study architecture.

Music was still very important to John. During his first 2 years at Texas Tech, John was able to go to school and keep on with his singing. He played with a rhythm-and-blues group and earned his spending money that way.

But in his third year at Texas Tech, John's interest in college began to lessen. As a result, his grades suffered. It was either music or school. John felt that he had to choose one or the other. He chose music. John knew that his decision would disappoint his parents. He was right. The Deutschendorfs were disappointed. Still they offered to help.

John had saved $125 from his performances on campus. His parents gave him the $250 they had put away for his tuition and told him he could use it in any way he wanted. John once told a reporter what his parents said, "We don't approve, but we'll always help you. If you get in trouble, call."

It was 1964, and John Deutschendorf headed for the West Coast, looking for places to sing. He took a job as a draftsman and played his guitar anywhere he could find an audience.

Folk music was big at that time. People would gather at various places for hootenannies and sing with a guitarist all evening. Yet it was difficult to find steady work at clubs. John said that he must have auditioned at every little club in Los Angeles.

Finally Randy Sparks hired John to sing at the Leadbetter Coffeehouse. John now laughs when he listens to some of the tapes of his shows at Leadbetter's. "They're the most boring thing you ever heard," he told a reporter with a grin. Randy Sparks helped John a great deal and showed him how to put a show together.

One night a producer heard John at Leadbetter's and asked him to audition for a record album. The producer also suggested that he change his name. It was too long for a record label, he said.

Of all the names suggested, John had a good feeling about only one of them — Denver. Denver meant mountains, streams, eagles soaring in the sky. Though John hadn't seen much of Denver, Colorado, he knew that the feeling in the name was right for him.

John was proud of the offer he had received to do a record album. He went home and told his family about it. However, when he returned to California, the producer wasn't interested any more. The album was never released. It was disappointing for John.

Luckily, a major opportunity came along. Chad Mitchell of the Chad Mitchell Trio decided to leave his folk group. The Trio needed a replacement. Over 250 persons tried out. Denver got the job.

"It was a very big step for me," John said later. "These guys were my idols, especially Chad . . . and here I was taking his place." Denver's first appearance with the Mitchell Trio was on July 4, 1965.

John feels that those years with the Mitchell Trio were eye-opening ones for him. He began to see the world in a larger way. He became more aware of the needs of people. He saw the power that sometimes harms people. He saw the evils of war and the constant danger of pollution. Soon these concerns became a vital part of the Trio's songs.

The Trio was an appealing group. There were always standing ovations for them at college concerts, yet only their concerts went well. The Trio's records never seemed to succeed.

In 1974 after John Denver became famous on his own, Mercury released a record called *Beginnings*, It had been recorded in 1965 by John and the other members of the Mitchell Trio. The sound is of high quality. But next to one of Denver's current albums, it really is a record from a different time.

John found two of the most important loves of his life while he was touring with the Mitchell Trio. He met Annie, his future wife. And he discovered Aspen, Colorado, the place of his future home.

John met Ann-Marie Martell in her home town, St.

Peter, Minnesota, in November, 1965. The Mitchell Trio was doing a concert at Gustavus Adolphus College in St. Peter during the school's campus charity week. After the concert John went to watch the various college clubs put on their shows to raise money for charity.

He remembered one girl in those shows especially well. She came on stage with different signs reading, "Act One," "Act Two," and "Applause." The girl was dressed in jeans and a red shirt, and, in John's words, "She looked so alive. I fell in love with her right then."

Though John was used to performing before large crowds, he was still very shy about meeting people — especially girls. He couldn't figure out how to meet this girl. As he stood there in the crowd, another girl asked him to sing. Annie joined in with the singing group, and John sang every song for her.

Nearly a year later in October, 1966, the Mitchell Trio was doing another concert in Minnesota, at Mankato State College. They had to drive through St. Peter to reach Mankato.

John told one of his friends about a girl he remembered from a year before. His friend was so surprised that John could remember one girl for a whole year that he found out Annie's phone number and gave it to John. Denver called her and invited her to his concert. She accepted. Two days later he asked her to another concert 50 miles away. Again she accepted.

John was in love. He would fly to St. Peter to see Annie between concerts. And if planes were grounded in bad weather, he'd take the train just to be with her for a day.

John spent the following Christmas with Annie and the Martell family in St. Peter. It was then he found out

that Annie and the college ski club were going to Aspen the following month. He decided to tag along and so discovered the second love of his life — Aspen.

The beauty of the mountains in Aspen overwhelmed John. Aspen was where he would like to live someday, somehow, and with Annie. On June 9, 1967, John Denver and Ann-Marie Martell were married in a formal ceremony in St. Peter.

Aspen didn't follow immediately. The couple lived in Chicago where John tried to get bookings for the Mitchell Trio.

Members in the Trio changed, and after awhile none of the original Trio remained. There were legal problems in using Chad Mitchell's name. So with Denver leading the group, they changed the name to "Denver, Boyce and Johnson." There were frequent arguments in the group, and the Trio had big debts. The Trio gave its last performance in November, 1968. They split up, and Denver was on his own.

John was glad to be on his own. He was tired of the many problems connected with groups. Still it was not easy. Denver had a wife to support. It was a difficult first year for the newly-married Denvers. And John had committed himself to paying off the Trio's debts.

Annie had married John at the end of her junior year in college. So in 1968 the couple moved back to Minnesota so that Ann could finish her degree in art education.

While John and Annie lived in Minneapolis, John often flew back to Aspen to look for singing jobs. He searched but couldn't find any. Finally at Christmastime in 1968, he was hired to play a week at a small club called the Leather Jug in Snowmass, near Aspen.

John did so well at the Leather Jug that the week

turned into a month. During that month the Aspen Winterskol festival was happening, and it included a songwriting contest. In about 15 minutes John wrote the song "Aspenglow." Though he didn't win the contest, his song may last longer than the one that did.

John's experience at the Leather Jug gave him the lift he needed. He was treated well by all the people. The spirit of skiers in the mountains made John feel that skiers were the friendliest people in the world.

Suddenly in 1969 John's singing took off with the ease of a skier schussing down a mountain. John contracted with colleges all over the country to do concerts. It was the year he wrote "Leaving, on a Jet Plane," one of the biggest hits of the year. After only one audition, RCA contracted with him to make albums. In 6 months John had paid off the Trio's debts.

In 1970 another part of John's dream came true. He and Annie moved to Aspen.

John creates songs out of his own life story. He uses his memories in song. He shares his concerns in song. He spreads his happiness to others in song.

John Denver tells a story in song so that the listeners will see their own life stories more clearly.

John Denver has been called "the minstrel of the mountains." He sings about the Rocky Mountains because they are an important part of his life. He has chosen to live near the mountains because he feels "high," he feels good about being there. It is one of his personal goals to preserve the mountains from pollution.

The environment never gets stale for Denver. The

A Man and His Environment

mountains keep changing, depending on the sun and shadows of each day.

The mountains accent the beauty of each season. In the winter sun John and Annie can spend days skiing. The green pines decorate the slopes. The winds blow snow from the pine branches and sprinkle it on the skiers. While riding up the ski lift, John has composed many songs. It was there that he wrote ''Annie's Song,'' a song which combines both his love for his wife and his love for the outdoors.

In the spring the mountains come alive with new life. Thick green moss outlines rushing streams. Wild flowers begin to appear. The evergreens take on a new, rich color.

In the summer and early fall the mountains are a place for camping, running and singing. It is a time when people can become a part of the mountains' life. John and Annie often backpack through the hills. They know the area well and enjoy new trails.

John has said that he loves performing even more than living in the Rocky Mountains; for, when he performs, he can take people back with him to the Rockies. It would be almost impossible to understand John Denver's recent music without understanding the place where he lives.

It was not until 2 years after John and Annie moved to Aspen that their home was completed. Just before Christmas of 1972, they moved into their 3-bedroom, split-level house. The house sits on 2½ acres of land in Starwood, Colorado, nearing the Roaring Fork River Valley. The Denvers can look out their windows and see the mountains all around them and the river right below.

When people come to see John, they might find him sitting in the glassed-in loft built into his roof. There he has time to think quietly or watch eagles through his

21

telescope.

There are beautiful green plants throughout the house. "It's Annie's green thumb that makes them thrive so well," her mother, Mrs. Martell, says. Annie is also a good cook. The Martells own a restaurant in St. Peter, which may have something to do with Annie's ability to cook. Annie says that John is "a cook's delight." He'll eat everything she prepares.

John and Annie both love animals. Their shaggy mutt, Murphy, is pictured with John on some of his album covers. Besides Murphy, the Denvers' other pets are Daisy, a Golden Retriever pup; Tiny Alice, a yellow cat; and Little Harriet, a gray cat.

John's interest in animals and in the Rockies made him interested in the plight of mountain sheep, called Bighorn. Bighorn sheep are being crowded off their ranges by cattle and horses in the United States and Canada.

Denver brought this concern to the public on a TV special early in 1973. John wrote and performed the music for the special and acted as narrator of the show. Denver made the show with Tommy Tompkins, a woodsman. In the show Tompkins teaches John about Bighorn sheep as the 2 men travel through Jasper and Banff National Parks in Canada. One reporter said that Denver's TV special on the Bighorn "established him with a sense of place and purpose that perhaps no other popular singer enjoys."

When John is home, he and Annie try to live as simply as possible. He has been called a creative, do-it-yourself man around the house. They have no maid, butler or gardener. Annie does her own cleaning, cooking and laundry.

John doesn't allow their home to be photographed and Annie prefers to stay out of the limelight. They both value privacy.

John makes going on the road as simple as possible, too. It's just a short trip from their home to the Aspen airport. He purchases tickets for his instruments so he won't have to worry about how they will be treated in the baggage compartment. John does what he can to keep hassles out of his career.

John sings about his feelings of being on the road in his album, *Back Home Again*. In "On the Road," he sings, "We didn't know who we were; we didn't know what we did. We were just on the road." John's been on the road. And John's been home. Both hold meaning for him.

Performer

"John Denver, RCA's recording artist, is a special talent who is on the threshold of stardom."
Billboard
April 18, 1970
Bitter End, N.Y.

Large trucks from Kearney, Nebraska, bring in John Denver's sound equipment. A crew sets it up. Sound men walk the stage, getting a feel for the different sides of the concert hall. "Too much of me, not enough of the bass," John calls as he tunes his guitar. Screens are set up behind John for slides and films. Testing before a concert is tedious but necessary work.

"John Denver is a troubadour in the truest sense of the word. Denver works appealingly on his own songs such as, 'Leaving on a Jet Plane,' and 'For

Baby,' and lends a distinctive interpretation to such titles as 'Going to Carolina'."
Billboard
November 14, 1970
The Troubadour, Los Angeles

John has trained his voice, though he has never had a voice lesson. His tenor voice has a broad sound rather than a nasal sound. His voice is clear and powerful. It's been said that his voice, smile and selection of songs have won him a following spanning all ages.

When everything is ready for a concert, John goes back to his dressing room and enjoys some quiet time by himself. Then it's time for the show to begin. Dressed in jeans, a western shirt and Cowboy boots, John walks on stage.

"We've got a far out show for you tonight." John's favorite expression is "far out." TV cameramen, stage-hands, and other musicians make bets on how many times John will say "far out" in an evening.

"Denver has the knack of being able to project the kind of living-room comfort which makes nightclub fans feel at home. The ample original material and excellent sense of humor enhance Denver's style."
Variety
May 21, 1969
Sheraton Ritz, Minneapolis

John Denver's concert performance is a gentle but gutsy one. John's image and songs are sincere but not simple.

Behind John, pictures of the Rockies and of mountain streams are projected on the screens. A steely-sounding rhythm comes from John's 12-string guitar. Mike Taylor on electric guitar and Dick Kniss on bass round out the

26

sound. In "Rocky Mountain High," John sings the story of what the mountains have done for his life.

Fans often ask Denver what "Rocky Mountain High" means. John says that he has had many different interpretations of the song offered to him. "But it is about my wife, and it says exactly what I want it to say; but I throw it out to you, and there it is." John tells his fans that they can make it mean whatever they want it to mean.

"Denver sings beautiful songs of love, peace and nature mixed in with clever satirical material."

Variety
August 19, 1970
Schaeffer Festival, N.Y. Central Park

In a performance John does a combination of his songs and other people's songs. He is more interested in singing songs that will touch people than he is in singing only the songs he has written. In choosing these songs, Denver looks for meaning as well as melody. His songs usually come from Tom Paxton, Paul McCartney, James Taylor and Jacques Brel.

"Denver combines a lucid voice that has personal quality with a relaxed, witty stage presence. His philosophy is: music is a life-style of people. He speaks of love, youth, hope, beauty. Denver is a friendly and whimsical performer."

Variety
April 15, 1970
Bitter End, N.Y.

Humor is strung through a John Denver concert. His jokes between songs are mild and always have a freshness about them. He encourages listeners to sing along but to keep to the choruses. "It's my show," he jokes. At a recent concert in Denver, John told his audience

Sunshine Singer

that he always wanted to be a country-western singer. So as a teenager, he would stand in front of a large mirror, practicing how to look "cool."

"RCA's hit, 'Take Me Home Country Roads,' coincided with West Virginia's booster campaign, 'Homecoming '71.' John Denver gave a command performance of his single to 10,000 at the statehouse grounds."

Billboard
August 29, 1971
Charleston, W. Va.

John Denver is a careful musician. He may not have a certain time set aside each day to practice, but he never lets a day go by without playing. He is his own critic and often says that his back-up musicians are more talented than he is.

John says that he is not a folk musician. Yet in the tradition of folk songs, he would like to see some of his songs last for awhile. One reporter has called Denver's songs his companions. They reflect John's thoughts on life as he walks through life. John classifies his music as contemporary. It is music of today.

Within one song John will often switch from a 6-string to a 12-string guitar. He always plays with at least another guitarist and a bass player. Sometimes a large orchestra appears with him at his concerts. The arrangements on "Rocky Mountain High" and on "Prisoners" reflect the jangly sound in much of today's music.

The mood and meaning are also of today. John's concerns with ecology and simple living show up in his songs. "Rhymes and Reasons" takes a look at the wisdom of children at a time when cities are crumbling.

"Sunshine On My Shoulder" suggests that sun can

be a way of getting high. "High" is sometimes associated with drugs. But for John, "high" means feeling good about yourself and about your surroundings.

John sings about what most people experience and think about. Anybody can identify with the sun, the season, the war, clean air or the outdoors.

"John Denver brought his self-styled folk songs of love, life and the great outdoors to an enthusiastically packed house."

> *Billboard*
> September 30, 1972
> Carnegie Hall, N.Y.

John has time for the crowds of teen-agers that wait for him after a show. He will sign autographs and talk with those that have questions and comments.

Denver recently was in London doing 6 shows for the British Broadcasting Company. In the 1973-74 TV season, John did 2 one-hour specials for ABC. He has frequently appeared on many other TV variety shows and has hosted Johnny Carson's "Tonight Show."

John Denver is easy about his fame. He doesn't push his success too far. No matter how many songs John Denver writes or how much money he makes, John's greatest rewards are in spreading joy as he performs. He listens to his audience almost more carefully than they listen to him. John Denver is a professional performer who makes an audience feel refreshed.

John says, "Somebody can come up to me tomorrow and say it's all over. And I'll say, 'It doesn't matter.' I'll go back to the Rocky Mountains and raise a family. Annie and I will put together a little restaurant. She'll cook, and I'll wait on tables and sing."

Then John adds, "And we'll be happy."

JACKSON FIVE
CARLY SIMON
BOB DYLAN
JOHN DENVER
THE BEATLES
ELVIS PRESLEY
JOHNNY CASH
CHARLEY PRIDE
ARETHA FRANKLIN
ROBERTA FLACK
STEVIE WONDER

Rock'n PopStars